87th
U. S. Open
Olympic Club

Writer
Larry Dennis

Photographers
Brian Morgan
Jim Moriarty

Editor
Bev Norwood

Assistant Editor
Jan Davis

ISBN 0-9615344-2-7

©1987 United States Golf Association®
Golf House, Far Hills, New Jersey 07931

Statistics produced by Unisys Corporation

Published by International Merchandising Corporation,
One Erieview Plaza, Cleveland, Ohio 44114

Printed in the United States of America

87th
U. S. Open
Official Annual Presented by
ROLEX

As probably every golf fan knows, The Olympic Club in San Francisco was the scene of a championship that I would just as soon forget. It was 1966, and I was leading by seven strokes with nine holes to play. Things began to turn around, Billy Casper tied me and won in a playoff the next day.

Yet, I have fond memories of Olympic and the gracious people there; I have always considered the course among the best in America. My entry was among the record 5,696 this year, and I would love to have played there again, but my game was not quite up to it.

As a television spectator for the eighty-seventh United States Open Championship, I thought it was another that will be remembered for a long time. It was inspiring to watch Tom Watson try to break out of his slump and, regardless of your sentiments, you had to admire the way Scott Simpson played, especially on the last five holes.

This annual is a worthy account of the championship and is the third in a series sponsored by my friends at Rolex to commemorate the United States Open. As in the past two years, proceeds from the sales through the USGA Associates Program will benefit junior golf in the USGA's on-going effort to promote the game.

We are all appreciative of your support.

Arnold Palmer

87th U.S. Open

June 18-21, 1987, Olympic Club (Lake Course), San Francisco, California

Contestant	Rounds	Total	Prize
Scott Simpson	71 68 70 68	277	$150,000.00
Tom Watson	72 65 71 70	278	75,000.00
Seve Ballesteros	68 75 68 71	282	46,240.00
Bobby Wadkins	71 71 70 71	283	24,542.80
Curtis Strange	71 72 69 71	283	24,542.80
Bernhard Langer	69 69 73 72	283	24,542.80
Ben Crenshaw	67 72 72 72	283	24,542.80
Larry Mize	71 68 72 72	283	24,542.80
Dan Pohl	75 71 69 69	284	15,004.20
Tsuneyuki Nakajima	68 70 74 72	284	15,004.20
Mac O'Grady	71 69 72 72	284	15,004.20
Jim Thorpe	70 68 73 73	284	15,004.20
Lennie Clements	70 70 70 74	284	15,004.20
Bob Eastwood	73 66 75 71	285	12,065.33
Isao Aoki	71 73 70 71	285	12,065.33
Tim Simpson	76 66 70 73	285	12,065.33
Jodie Mudd	72 75 71 68	286	9,747.28
Jim Woodward	71 74 72 69	286	9,747.28
Mark Calcavecchia	73 68 73 72	286	9,747.28
David Frost	70 72 71 73	286	9,747.28
Masashi Ozaki	71 69 72 74	286	9,747.28
Nick Price	69 74 69 74	286	9,747.28
Kenny Knox	72 71 69 74	286	9,747.28
Don Pooley	74 72 72 69	287	7,719.71
Jay Don Blake	70 75 71 71	287	7,719.71
Steve Pate	71 72 72 72	287	7,719.71
Craig Stadler	72 68 74 73	287	7,719.71
Danny Edwards	72 70 72 73	287	7,719.71
Peter Jacobsen	72 71 71 73	287	7,719.71
John Mahaffey	72 72 67 76	287	7,719.71
Ken Green	71 74 75 68	288	6,554.60
Tony Sills	71 70 75 72	288	6,554.60
Hal Sutton	74 70 70 74	288	6,554.60
Dale Douglass	70 73 69 76	288	6,554.60
Keith Clearwater	74 71 64 79	288	6,554.60
Scott Hoch	72 70 77 70	289	5,626.00
Sandy Lyle	70 74 72 73	289	5,626.00
Lanny Wadkins	73 71 72 73	289	5,626.00
Denis Watson	69 74 72 74	289	5,626.00
Rodger Davis	75 68 72 74	289	5,626.00
Barry Jaeckel	73 70 72 74	289	5,626.00
John Cook	70 68 76 75	289	5,626.00
Sam Randolph	71 71 76 72	290	4,856.66
Raymond Floyd	68 73 76 73	290	4,856.66
Wayne Grady	73 70 74 73	290	4,856.66
Roger Maltbie	73 73 75 70	291	4,240.00
Ralph Landrum	72 71 74 74	291	4,240.00
Fred Couples	72 71 73 75	291	4,240.00

Contestant	Rounds	Total	Prize
Tom Kite	76 69 70 76	291	4,240.00
Jack Nicklaus	70 68 76 77	291	4,240.00
Joey Sindelar	75 71 75 71	292	3,462.14
David Hobby	77 70 73 72	292	3,462.14
Gil Morgan	72 71 76 73	292	3,462.14
David Graham	71 76 72 73	292	3,462.14
Ed Dougherty	73 67 78 74	292	3,462.14
Greg Norman	72 69 74 77	292	3,462.14
Mark McCumber	72 72 69 79	292	3,462.14
Bob Lohr	76 67 79 71	293	3,178.00
Duffy Waldorf	74 69 75 75	293	3,178.00
Mike Smith	73 71 74 75	293	3,178.00
Eddie Kirby	73 69 75 76	293	3,178.00
Jack Renner	73 73 71 76	293	3,178.00
Mark Wiebe	70 67 77 79	293	3,178.00
Gene Sauers	72 69 73 79	293	3,178.00
Bob Gilder	72 72 70 79	293	3,178.00
Russ Cochran	71 69 81 73	294	3,165.00
Mark McNulty	73 72 73 76	294	3,165.00
Tom Purtzer	74 73 77 71	295	3,165.00
Jose Maria Olazabal	76 69 76 74	295	3,165.00
Bob Tway	70 71 79 75	295	3,165.00
Donnie Hammond	75 71 76 74	296	3,165.00
Jim Carter	75 72 75 74	296	3,165.00
Gary Hallberg	71 72 69 85	297	3,165.00
David Ogrin	74 72 74 78	298	3,165.00
Dave Eichelberger	72 75 77 76	300	3,165.00
Fred Wadsworth	75 71 77 77	300	3,165.00
David Rummells	74 73 76 78	301	3,165.00

Paul Azinger	76-72—148	Kirk Triplett	75-74—149	*Buddy Alexander	76-77—153
John Morse	74-74—148	Bart Bryant	75-75—150	Roy Biancalana	78-76—154
Ernie Gonzalez	72-76—148	John Grund	76-74—150	David Canipe	79-75—154
Doug Tewell	75-73—148	Bill Buttner	72-78—150	D.A. Weibring	77-77—154
Robert Wrenn	74-74—148	Darrell Kestner	73-77—150	Andy Bean	74-80—154
Joey Rassett	75-73—148	Hale Irwin	79-71—150	Scott Steger	77-77—154
Kevin Klier	76-72—148	Brandel Chamblee	73-77—150	Steve Brady	77-77—154
Payne Stewart	74-74—148	Chip Beck	77-74—151	Bill Bergin	73-81—154
Mark Lye	78-70—148	Mike Reid	74-77—151	Frank Conner	79-75—154
Gary Krueger	74-74—148	Larry Nelson	76-75—151	Mark Brooks	79-75—154
Scott Hazledine	77-71—148	Lee Trevino	73-78—151	Alan Tapie	78-77—155
Mike Nicolette	76-72—148	Bill Britton	77-74—151	Griffin Rudolph	77-78—155
Johnny Miller	71-77—148	Scott Verplank	78-73—151	Mike Miles	79-76—155
Mike Donald	76-72—148	Mark Aebli	75-76—151	Jerry Haas	75-80—155
Jim White	76-72—148	Bill Glasson	77-75—152	Mark O'Meara	76-79—155
Andy North	74-74—148	Fuzzy Zoeller	78-74—152	Jon Kudysch	84-72—156
Steve Gotsche	72-76—148	Bob Lunn	75-77—152	Larry Emery	79-77—156
Calvin Peete	73-75—148	Ivan Smith	74-78—152	Jeff Maggert	79-78—157
Don Bies	76-73—149	Jim Booros	76-76—152	Brian Fogt	77-80—157
Mike Hulbert	73-76—149	Gary Pinns	74-78—152	Loren Roberts	79-78—157
Brian Tennyson	75-74—149	Gary Koch	77-75—152	Joel Edwards	81-78—159
Jim Colbert	76-73—149	Hubert Green	77-75—152	Charles Bolling	81-79—160
Tom Lehman	77-72—149	Jay Overton	78-74—152	Norm Becker	83-77—160
Fred Funk	74-75—149	*Greg Parker	77-76—153	Adam Adams	77-84—161
T.C. Chen	75-74—149	Greg Powers	76-77—153	Robert Gaona	86-76—162
Patrick Horgan	76-73—149	Robert Boyd	83-70—153	Corey Pavin	WD
				Dave Barr	72- WD

Professionals not returning 72-hole scores received $600 each.   *Denotes amateur.

87th U. S. Open

Olympic Club

Great things have happened at Olympic in the past. It's got some magic about it, and I like to see the Open go where there's some magic.

Frank Hannigan

Ever since the eventual site was granted to a corporal in the Mexican militia in 1835, strange things have been happening at The Olympic Club's golf courses.

Rancho Laguna de la Merced covered half a league of windswept sandhills from the Pacific Ocean to Lake Merced on the southwestern edge of San Francisco. Mexico owned all of California then, and Corporal Jose Antonio Galindo convinced the authorities the land was "barren and useless, almost worthless, and fit only for pasture." So they sold it to him for $4.

Two years later Galindo sold the land to Francisco de Haro for one hundred cows and $25 in goods, at the time a profit worthy of an extortionist. Not long after, Jose was arrested and jailed for murder.

The property has since been owned by a water company, leased by a private club that went bankrupt and, finally, bought by a club that was founded to build muscles, not putting strokes.

It is a country club at which three United States Opens now have been played....on the wrong course! For a long time, the club couldn't even figure out who designed its courses.

Olympic is where, in the 1940s, Ty Cobb lost in the club tournament to a junior member named Bob Rosburg and walked out in a huff, never to return. It is where Jack Nicklaus had to pull off a near-miracle to beat a five-handicap member in an even-up match. It is where Ben Hogan got beat out of a record fifth Open by a club pro from Iowa and where Arnold Palmer beat himself out of a second Open title.

It is no wonder that when the United States Golf Association scheduled its 1987 national championship at Olympic, folks began pondering what could possibly happen this time.

Olympic is a fun place, a decidedly unsnooty place that's the antithesis of the typical — and erroneous — country club image. The membership is mostly upper-middle-class businessmen, considered a microcosm of San Francisco itself.

It is a club in which members sit in the sprawling, tan, stucco clubhouse, play dominoes — a singularly San Francisco custom — and roll the dice for drinks. There is an Irish corner, which recently has admitted some Italians, one of the many little alcoves in the men's locker room that originally were built for the members to better hide their liquor during Prohibition.

The average age is fifty-two, young by country club standards, and the raucousness has diminished over the years. One thing that has not changed is the golf. With a couple of the world's fine courses at their disposal, Olympic members are golfers. There are 212 with single-digit handicaps, twenty-five at scratch or one.

There are no starting times at Olympic, and you can always get a game. Be prepared to play in the rain, and don't complain. Get soaking wet, hole out, go in and have a drink.

Two Olympic members — Ken Venturi and Johnny Miller — have won the U.S. Open and another, Rosburg, has won the PGA Championship.

But the best golfer Olympic ever had, considering more than just ball-striking ability, may have been the late Johnny Swanson, who operated a bowling alley. He's a legend at the club, and the best story comes from his meeting with Nicklaus when Jack was traveling to Pebble Beach in 1961, on his way to winning the U.S. Amateur there.

Swanson, carrying a five handicap at the time, arranged a match with Nicklaus, former *San Francisco Examiner* golf writer Nelson Cullenward and Bob Callan, a 22-year-old law student who would go on to win the club championship four times (and lose it five times). Callan also has been the club president

Opposite page, Hole 8, par 3, 132 yards.
Above, Hole 3, par 3, 223 yards.

and a member of Olympic's 1987 Open Executive Committee.

Let Nicklaus, who became great friends with Swanson, tell the story:

"I asked John how many strokes he wanted. He looked at me with that smirk he always had and said, 'Strokes? Listen, fat boy, I don't need anything from you. It's you and me, belly to belly, for all your trophies.' You know, I had to eagle the seventeenth to keep from losing."

It took a few transplanted golfers, of course, to make all this hilarity possible. The first was John Lawson, who had prospered in San Francisco after arriving from Scotland. Out for a horseback ride south of town in 1906, he quickly sized up the land, then owned by the Spring Valley Water Company, as natural ground for a golf course.

That led to the formation of the Lakeside Golf Club, which leased part of the water company's tract and hired Wilfred Reid, a prominent English golf professional, architect and *bon vivant*, to design a challenging course on the sandhills. Reid completed the job in 1917, and for the next seventy years he was the man generally credited with designing Olympic.

At the time, The Olympic Club was strictly a downtown athletic club, founded in a firehouse in 1860 and destined to become one of the best-known athletic institutions in the world. Now the 8,000 members use their huge, brick downtown headquarters for fitness, swimming, racquet sports and the like. Across town, at ocean's edge, about 1,000 of those members play golf.

Shortly after World War I, the Lakeside Club was in financial trouble and the Spring Valley Company couldn't decide what to do with its land. Olympic members wanted another game to play, so they took over the golf course, later exercising an option to buy it. With the deal came the club professional, Sam Whiting, who at one time ranked among the best players in England and the Continent.

The Olympic Club decided it needed two courses to accommodate its membership and destroyed the Reid layout, which nobody liked much anyway. William Watson, another noted designer, was called in and teamed with Whiting, who was named superintendent of construction.

According to Bill Callan and Jim Innis, a couple of current Olympic members who

Hole 11, par 4, 430 yards.

have spent eons digging through old files to document the club's history, Watson probably left for other pastures after the blueprints were completed. It then became Whiting's job to remove Reid's course and convert the rest of the wild, thicket-covered dunes and hills into playable holes.

The Lake Course and the Pacific Links were opened in 1924. Now known as the Ocean Course, the Pacific Links was intended to be Olympic's signature layout — "the St. Andrews of America" — with ten of its holes built along the dunes west of Skyline Drive, a highway separating the rest of the club from the ocean.

In 1925, however, heavy winter rains caused a landslide that wiped out eight of the ocean holes and forced Whiting to rebuild both courses. Most of the new holes were constructed away from the ocean, eliminating much of the links look and feel. When the new courses were ready for play in 1927, the Lake had become the standard-bearer.

Despite a history troubled by sinkage that now has cost it all its seaside holes, the pretty ocean course today is still preferred by many members over its more famous sister.

In 1927, the two new courses were still treeless dunesland layouts. So Whiting, citing the need to protect the members from the wind, planted trees — lots of trees, some 30,000 to 40,000, depending on whose count you believe. He planted cypress, cedar, pine, oak, eucalyptus and even redwood, a tree not found on your everyday golf course. And the trees grew. . . .and grew, taller and wider, eventually closing in the fairways and giving the course its distinctive parkland-on-the-sea look. It also sharpened the tempers of members who kept — and keep — banging balls off them or, worse, into them, never to be found again.

The trees were to be a factor in the 1987 Open, with rather expensive consequences in a couple of cases.

What Whiting created — with a nod to Watson — was a masterpiece of beauty, variety and difficulty, a course whose holes twist and turn through the woodland, pitching and rolling up and down those once-exposed dunes. The greens are mostly smallish and sloping, devilish when cut close. The lengths range from the 609-yard sixteenth to the 132-yard eighth. There is a 288-yard par-

Hole 15, par 3, 149 yards.

four, the seventh, innocuous in distance but with a green that can leave you dazed. And the 343-yard eighteenth, downhill and then uphill to a treacherous green, is one of the world's great finishing holes. And mostly there are just a lot of long, hard par-fours.

Olympic was the site of the 1930, 1932 and 1939 Match Play Open and the San Francisco Open in 1946, when Bryon Nelson beat a field that included Ben Hogan and Jimmy Demaret.

Hogan was to return in 1955, when the club was awarded the first of its U.S. Opens, and it was not to be an enjoyable visit.

To prepare for that Open, Olympic summoned Robert Trent Jones, who was twenty years into a career that has seen him design and redesign more golf courses than any architect ever.

Jones lengthened the course, tightened it, removed all but one of the fairway bunkers and added others around the greens. He changed the seventh from a kitten to a tiger by adding greenside bunkering and a crown contour in the center of the putting surface. And he changed the par-five seventeenth into an exacting par four for the championship, where it has remained for every ensuing USGA championship. The members, thankfully, always go to the back tee and play it as a par five. Open competitors, to their dismay, don't have that option.

When Hogan arrived in 1955, he found the course custom-made. The greens were glassy and the thick, clumpy Italian rye rough was a foot deep in areas off the target zone. Hogan, who could perhaps control the ball better than anybody who ever played the game, loved it.

Jack Fleck, the Iowan who was head professional at Duck Creek Golf Club in Davenport and the Credit Island driving range in Bettendorf, didn't like it so well. He shot 87 in a practice round. But it was the rough that was to bring Hogan, not Fleck, to grief.

Hogan led the Open by a stroke at 217 after a 72 on Saturday's morning round, back when they played thirty-six holes on the final day. Fleck, having recovered from his practice debacle, was at 220. Then Ben apparently dispatched the competition with an even-par 70

Opposite page, Hole 18, par 4, 343 yards.

in the afternoon for a total of 287, seven over par.

But it wasn't to be good enough for Hogan. Fleck needed to birdie two of the last four holes to tie. He did, making birdie at the fifteenth and sinking a seven-footer for birdie on the eighteenth.

In the playoff the next day, Fleck went three strokes ahead at one point, but Hogan had cut the deficit to one at the eighteenth. Then his foot slipped, his drive went left into the knee-deep rough and he took three shots to get out. Fleck, with an easy par at that point, had denied history.

In 1958, Charlie Coe won the U.S. Amateur at Olympic, and in 1966 the Open returned. Arnold Palmer, still one of the game's dominant players at the time, had his second Open championship in his pocket, leading by seven over Billy Casper with nine holes to play. He was six under par for the championship and needed only to shoot a one-over-par 36 on the incoming nine to break Ben Hogan's record of 276. So, in typical Palmer fashion, he refused to play safe and went for every flag.

Instead he kept finding rough, especially on the long sixteenth. There he made a bogey —and it was a good bogey too — that, coupled with Casper's birdie, reduced the lead to one. That evaporated when Arnold missed a relatively short uphill putt for par on the seventeenth. Palmer, the charger, left it short.

Palmer saved the tie with a gutty five-foot par putt on the eighteenth, and he actually led the Monday playoff by two strokes after nine. But it seemed almost pre-ordained that he would lose. He bogeyed the eleventh, fourteenth and fifteenth holes and double-bogeyed the sixteenth coming in to shoot 73. Casper, with a 69, had dethroned the king.

Fifteen years later, in 1981, The Olympic Club members decided they were again ready to play host to a national championship, this time the U.S. Amateur. In that one, Nathaniel Crosby found a place in the sun for the first and — so far — only time in his career.

As the Open approached again, Frank Hannigan, Senior Executive Director of the USGA, was saying, "Great things have happened at Olympic in the past. It's got some magic about it, and I like to see the Open go where there's some magic."

87th U. S. Open

Prologue

It's a dynamite course. It makes you hit the shots. If you don't, it will kill you.

Tom Kite

You can eliminate three-quarters of the field on a course like this.

Fuzzy Zoeller

Who can you count out? I think Keith Clearwater could win. I think I could win. There are a lot of guys out here who have the ability to win.

Scott Simpson

Golfers are getting bigger, stronger and better. They practice more, work out in the gym and pay more attention to their health habits. Which helps them hit the ball farther and more consistently.

There also are more of them. The depth of quality players in the world has never been greater.

As the stars we grew up with grow older, the Big Three or Four or Five has become the Big 100. A whole lot of folks out there can win. . . .and do.

That is not always true at a U.S. Open, where the United States Golf Association sets up conditions that establish par as a standard. There will be no twenty unders, thank you. And the pressure of playing for the national championship eliminates some. There have been some unheralded winners, but the champion generally is a quality player. It's just that the list of those is getting longer.

When the field of 156 players, those remaining from the original 5,696 entries, arrived at The Olympic Club in the third week of June for the eighty-seventh renewal of the championship, they found a typical Open course. . .and maybe more.

At the start of the week, when sunny and windy and reasonably warm conditions prevailed, the greens at this venerable San Fran-cisco club were firm and fast, as were the fairways. But the demon rough that had entrapped Ben Hogan and Arnold Palmer and cost them championships — and indeed had been as high as six inches, thick and wet, just a month before — had been mowed to a more manageable four inches. There were few complaints from the contestants.

Jack Nicklaus said the course was "monotonous — there is no water, no out-of-bounds; you just plod along and play golf." That was translated in the newspapers as "boring," which was not fair to Nicklaus. But even "monotonous" was an opinion not shared by the field.

"It's a dynamite course," said Tom Kite. "It makes you hit the shots. If you don't, it will kill you."

Said 1983 champion Larry Nelson, "I think it's the best Open course I've ever seen. It's like a fairyland, one of those courses you just love to play."

Ben Crenshaw called it a "pure golf course, well-balanced and full of subtleties."

Greg Norman said, "The golf course is as good as I've ever seen set up."

But if this were a love affair, it was a precarious one.

Despite its relative lack of length — at 6,709 yards, the Lake Course was the shortest Open venue since Merion in 1981 — predictions were that the longer hitters would be favored. Hogan called Olympic "the longest short course in the world," with justification. It has eight par-four holes 417 yards or longer and a 609-yard par-five. The fairways for the championship were firm and close-cut, affording some roll, but the roll was often sideways on Olympic's slanting terrain, and that compounded the problem. On the seventeenth, with its severe left-to-right slope, it was especially difficult to keep even an accurate drive from tumbling downhill into the rough. "There's not a green on the course as fast as

the seventeenth fairway," Nicklaus declared.

"If you had a 7,200-yard course that played as long as this one, we'd never finish," said Fuzzy Zoeller.

The winner also would be one with steady nerves and an accurate putter. The smallish greens, many severely canted, were beautifully smooth but incredibly slick, as the USGA demands. Early in the week the report was that they were measuring thirteen feet on the Stimpmeter. For the uninitiated, that's like trying to putt down a marble staircase and stop the ball on the third step from the bottom. Particularly terrifying were the third, seventeenth and seventh, the latter a three-tiered green — from the top level, it was impossible early in the week to stop the ball on the middle tier. Efforts were being made to slow those down.

Morever, few of the players were familiar with the course, its undulations and the wind that swirls devilishly through the trees.

So an air of trepidation hung over Olympic, replacing for the moment the relentless San Francisco fog. The players were tip-toeing warily around the course, waiting for it to strike back at any moment. "Playing holes three, four, five and six is like walking through a minefield," said Crenshaw.

Most were looking at even-par 280 as the winning score.

Raymond Floyd, the defender, predicted somewhere between 290 and 300 if the sun stayed out and the wind kept blowing, further firming the fairways and making the greens hard and crusty.

"You can eliminate three-quarters of the field on a course like this," Zoeller remarked. "It's a fun course to play, but you have to work your butt off. You have to get the ball in the right areas of the fairways to get it on the green in the right places.

"It takes patience. You don't want to hit the little red button too early."

Patience.

It's a word that was to be heard often in the coming days.

The 1987 season had been relatively serene to this point. Norman had been shocked out of his second consecutive major championship

Opposite page, defending champion Raymond Floyd. Above, Tom Watson
(left) and Jack Nicklaus in a practice round that was beneficial to both.

when Larry Mize chipped in on the second hole of the Masters playoff, topping Bob Tway's hole-out from the bunker on the seventy-second hole of last year's PGA Championship. Other than that, it had been pretty much business as usual for the touring professionals. There had been four first-time winners, a typical allotment. Paul Azinger had won both his first and second events, joining Corey Pavin as the only multiple winners, and rested atop the money list with $450,462.

Rookie Keith Clearwater had shot two remarkable 64s in a Sunday double-round to win at Colonial, possibly a portent.

Some of the old boys had come out of hibernation; Johnny Miller, George Burns, Don Pooley and J. C. Snead all won tournaments after lengthy droughts. Payne Stewart finally shrugged off his runner-up status with victory at Bay Hill. And Tom Kite rolled along, winning for the seventh consecutive year.

Scott Simpson, in the midst of a successful but unremarkable career, won the Greater Greensboro Open, his third victory since he joined the PGA Tour in 1979. He was ninth in the money rankings with $315,896, already his best year ever.

The foreign invaders were still attacking the financial beachheads regularly. Norman, the Australian who won ten tournaments worldwide, including the British Open, in 1986, was without a U.S. triumph in 1987, although he won the Australian Masters early in the year. Spain's Seve Ballesteros, an infrequent visitor to this country who has won three major titles, had won once in 1987 in Europe, as had Bernhard Langer, the German who won the 1985 Masters. All were among the favorites.

Britain's Sandy Lyle; South Africa's Mark McNulty (a six-time winner in 1987) and David Frost; Nick Price and Denis Watson of Zimbabwe; and Japan's Tsuneyuki (Tommy) Nakajima, Masashi (Jumbo) Ozaki, and Isao Aoki were also among the foreign threats.

Others highly regarded included straight-shooting Lanny Wadkins, the ever-contending Stewart, Kite, Crenshaw, Pavin and Hal Sut-

*Opposite page, favorite Greg Norman makes a point with caddy
Pete Bender. Above, Paul Azinger entered the Open with two victories.*

Larry Mize was a focus of attention as the Masters champion.

ton, all of whom, except Sutton, the 1983 PGA champion, had won tournaments in 1987. Mize was getting some consideration, as was Mark Calcavecchia, a tournament winner.

Floyd had been strangely quiet after perhaps his best year ever, resting in sixty-second place on the money list with only two top-ten finishes and five missed cuts to show for thirteen starts. He was getting only cautious consideration, as was young Tway, the 1986 PGA Tour Player of the Year, and Zoeller, the 1984 Open winner, both having mediocre years.

At one point, Simpson quietly declared that fifty or sixty players could win. "Who can you count out?" he asked. "I think Keith Clearwater could win. I think I could win. There are a lot of guys out here who have the ability to win."

Tom Watson, trying to find a swing plane that worked, and Nicklaus, struggling to find anything that worked, were not expected to contend for the title.

Watson had not won since 1984. Nicklaus, who had played in only seven tournaments in 1987, said, "I'm playing as badly right now as I can ever remember playing. I can't hit the ball square on the clubface, and I don't know why."

On Wednesday, at a dinner given by the USGA for the Golf Writers Association of America, Watson was presented the prestigious Bob Jones Award for sportsmanship. The award was given in tandem by two long-time Watson friends, Frank D. (Sandy) Tatum, Jr., former president of the USGA, and Byron Nelson, himself a recipient of the award and Watson's primary teacher the last dozen years.

In Tom's case, the award was not so much for a single act during the previous year, but for a career of sportsmanship and strict adherence to the rules.

During his acceptance speech, Watson recounted some of his personal highlights but remarked at one point that he wasn't one to dwell on what he had accomplished. "I've always felt you should let your sticks do your talking," he said. There was a touch of wistfulness to it. Watson's sticks hadn't been saying much lately.

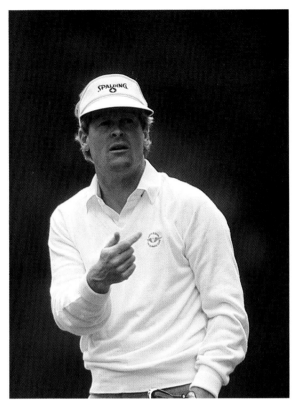

Local favorite Johnny Miller.

Amateur champion Buddy Alexander.

International stars Mark McNulty (left) and Masashi Ozaki.

I can't describe to you what important championships mean to me. To have done it once is tremendous, and I'd love to do it again.

Ben Crenshaw

It was a round you dream about, something I didn't expect, although I knew I was playing well.

Raymond Floyd

Maybe I can push my way through a major championship on adrenaline.

Jack Nicklaus

When Thursday came, the fog had returned and the skies were gray and cool. In an act of charity, the United States Golf Association had ordered the greens watered for two five-minute periods Wednesday night and the mowers had been raised for the extra-slick seventeenth and eighteenth greens. When the wind died and the clouds rolled in, the putting surfaces retained their moisture and the condition of the course was dramatically changed. Shots were now holding, Stimpmeter green speed was at a less-terrifying eleven feet and The Olympic Club had lost some of its bite.

Ben Crenshaw, who loves old golf books and old golf courses, was the first to take advantage. Benefitting from an early tee time, he cruised around in three-under-par 67, although the journey was not without some of Ben's usual mishaps. Through thirteen holes he was four under par after short-putt birdies at the third and fourth and two "no-brainers," a sixty-footer at the eleventh and a thirty-five-foot downhill putt at the thirteenth, both of which he admitted he was simply trying to get close.

At the fourteenth, a 417-yard par-four that now doglegs left after an altering of the fair-

Opposite page, Ben Crenshaw started with 67 for the first-round lead.

way, Crenshaw found the rough with his drive and a bunker with his second. He "misread the sand," fluffed his bunker shot short of the green, pitched to five feet and missed the putt. Double-bogey.

Crenshaw, a gentle but emotional man, in the past might have given it all away at that point. Instead, he parred the fifteenth, then saved the round with cool play on the 609-yard sixteenth. His second shot found the left rough behind a tree, so Crenshaw chipped back to the fairway, struck an eighty-seven-yard wedge shot five feet from the hole and sank for his par. He barely missed a twelve-foot birdie putt on the fearsome seventeenth, then birdied the tricky little eighteenth from three feet.

The lead would hold up through the day, but the challengers would be many and significant. Something very strange was going on. For the first time in recent memory, every name on the leaderboard was recognizable. No unknowns were in sight this Open, nor would they be.

Instead, Crenshaw faced familiar threats, albeit some a bit surprising. Seve Ballesteros got in at 68. No surprise there. So did Tommy Nakajima, and that was no shocker, either. Nakajima is a world-class player who contends often in major championships, although he has yet to win one.

Raymond Floyd lifted some eyebrows when he snapped out of his lackluster play, hit sixteen greens in regulation, made no bogeys and also posted a two-under score in a round he said was his finest since the last day of last year's Open.

"It was a round you dream about, something I didn't expect, although I knew I was playing well," said the 1986 winner at Shinnecock Hills, who admitted his relatively poor season to date was due to neglect more than anything else.

"Being the reigning champion has been a tremendous experience," Floyd said. "I've

Senior Open champion Dale Douglass (above) had a strong performance. Opposite page, Seve Ballesteros at 68 was one stroke behind.

smelled the roses. But I did not put in the hours on my game as I have during my career. I've been busting my butt for twenty-four years, and after winning the Open I was determined I was going to have some fun. My short game has enabled me to have a great career, but I didn't work on it the last few months like I should have."

Then Floyd smiled tightly and said, "But I gave myself time to work before this tournament."

Denis Watson, whose two-stroke penalty in the 1985 Open at Oakland Hills — he waited too long for a putt to drop — left him one shot back in that championship, shot 69, as did Nick Price and Bernhard Langer.

First Round	
Ben Crenshaw	67
Seve Ballesteros	68
Tommy Nakajima	68
Raymond Floyd	68
Denis Watson	69
Nick Price	69
Bernhard Langer	69

Ten were tied at 70. Included were Jay Don Blake (well, okay, allow us one unknown, but at least he's a member of the PGA Tour), Lennie Clements, David Frost, Mark Wiebe, Sandy Lyle, Bob Tway, John Cook and Jim Thorpe, who seems to play well on courses where a hot putter is not the key to the kingdom.

Also at par was Dale Douglass, the personable U.S. Senior Open champion. . . ."I'm just preparing for the big one in three weeks," he cracked.

And, just to remind everyone that this was indeed the U.S. Open, here came Jack Nicklaus in at even par.

He has won four of these championships, the last in 1980, and sixteen other major titles. And every time he is pronounced dead, he jumps up and wins another, as in 1986 at the Masters.

This time Nicklaus had virtually pronounced himself dead, but the juices began to flow as they always do for him at major championship time, the putter began to work better and he was once again in the hunt.

Nicklaus had, humiliatingly, missed the cut the week before at Westchester and on Tuesday of Open week was "never more down on myself." But changes were in the offing. He had won the Masters with an oversized putter and had put his old, short-bladed model on the shelf with his fishing gear. But a tip from Denis Watson, who advised that every once in a while it was necessary to go back to a smaller putter to regain feel, especially on lightning-fast greens, led him to retrieve the old faithful.

"I was getting too mechanical with the big putter," Nicklaus explained. "With the small blade you get more feel in the fingers, although for a while it felt like I was hitting a volleyball with a pencil."

Nicklaus also went back to his old putting method, striking the ball with the bottom of the blade, almost topping it, a style that rolls the putts well if properly executed.

Nicklaus had cold-topped two three-wood shots at Westchester — "I'll bet even you guys don't top more than one a round," he told the assembled press earlier

Raymond Floyd had an opening 68.

in the week. Some swing changes obviously were called for.

"I'd been manufacturing everything I was doing," Jack said. "I discovered Tuesday I had my arms outstretched with tension, and you can't play golf with tension in your arms. So I started to just let them hang."

Things started to get better immediately. On Wednesday, Nicklaus played with Tom Watson, each commiserating with the other's recent travail. They later agreed that the round and the conversation probably was good for both of them.

On Thursday, Nicklaus began holing some confidence-inducing putts and the swing was still improving.

"As I walked down the tenth fairway, I almost felt like I knew what I was doing, and that's a nice feeling," he said.

On the fifteenth, he struck a seven-iron to within fifteen feet and made the putt for a birdie, then hit a seven-iron third shot on the sixteenth to twenty feet and made that.

"It was," he said afterward, "somebody I'm not familiar with."

Despite a three-putt bogey on the eighteenth, Nicklaus remained optimistic. "I'm still not hitting the ball well," he said, "but I'm hitting it with some idea of what is happening. I didn't hit anything I couldn't find, and don't laugh. I've hit some lately I had trouble finding.

"If I keep progressing, I should be around. I'm not close to being as good as I was, but when I get to a major I get myself pumped up. Maybe I can push my way through a major championship on adrenaline."

Watson also showed some signs of life. He got in at 72 after holing a bunker shot for birdie on the seventeenth. "That was a big shot," he said, "because I went from three over to two over when I could have gone four over."

Johnny Miller, the local favorite who played in his first Open at Olympic as a 19-year-old amateur in 1966 —and finished tied for eighth, was challenging for the lead at two under par through sixteen holes. Then he finished double-bogey, bogey for 71, still respectable but disappointing. "They should rename golf," he said. "Could have been, should have been."

The list of fifteen players at 71 included Mac O'Grady, considered perhaps the best ball-striker on Tour but so suspect with the

Opposite page, Tommy Nakajima was also in the second-place grouping.

putter that he does it lefthanded; Larry Mize, the only man left with a chance at the Grand Slam; former U.S. Amateur champion Sam Randolph and Scott Simpson.

Mize salvaged his round with the day's best shot. On the eighteenth, he pulled his second into heavy rough above the left bunker. Looking at a hole set in the bottom center of the severely slanting, dished-in green, Mize lobbed a pitch some twenty feet above the hole. The ball rolled to the far side, almost getting caught in the fringe there, then turned and slid back to within a foot of the cup.

Simpson played a solid round, offsetting bogeys at the first, fourteenth and seventeenth with birdies on the short eighth and fifteenth.

Greg Norman was still in the chase despite bogeys at the twelfth, thirteenth and fourteenth.

He was among twenty players at 72, a group that included John Mahaffey, Craig Stadler and Dave Barr.

Lanny Wadkins was the first to run afoul of Olympic's ball-eating trees. His tee shot on the ninth found a cypress to the right of the fairway, and the tree wouldn't give it up. Wadkins, who could have climbed after it, opted to re-tee. He made a double-bogey and finished with 73.

The trees were to have their way three more times in the championship, with Sandy Lyle and Nakajima on Saturday and Floyd on the final day. As it turned out, Nakajima was the most seriously victimized.

Payne Stewart, another of the early favorites, was cruising along nicely until he four-putted the seventeenth and three-putted the eighteenth to shoot 74.

Bernhard Langer (left) was in good position after his 69, but Hal Sutton never recovered from his first-round 74.

Calvin Peete also had a four-putt, on the fifth green, and shot 73.

Tom Kite, considered a good bet after his victory two weeks earlier at the Kemper Open, struggled to a 76, as did Larry Nelson and Paul Azinger. Fuzzy Zoeller, full of aches and pains, reported in at 78.

Corey Pavin, who had spent two weeks preparing for the Open, injured his back in the practice round Wednesday and withdrew after seven holes.

Crenshaw immediately became the sentimental favorite of many. Now 35 and in his fourteenth full season as a professional, he has had a career marked by several peaks, including the 1984 Masters title, and many valleys, including a divorce and a thyroid problem that debilitated him in 1985.

Now he was on the trail of another major championship, and it was a different Crenshaw in the hunt. He has remarried and his wife, Julie, is expecting their first child. Once known as much for his terrible temper on the golf course as his sweet disposition off it, Ben was bringing maturity and a new composure to the hunt. And he knew what was needed in the days ahead.

"I'm one of those people who said don't do anything dumb on this course," he said. "I'm more patient than I was. I'm trying to approach golf from a more common-sense nature. I've let my emotions get away from me in major championships, and that's something I'll always work on.

"Everyone knows I'm on the historical side. I can't describe to you what important championships mean to me. To have done it once is tremendous, and I'd love to do it again."

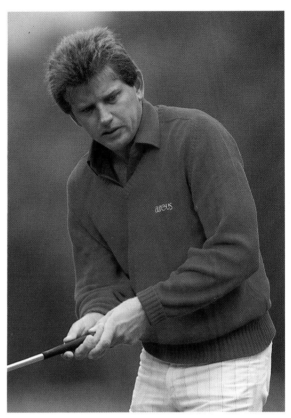

Zimbabwe's Denis Watson (left) and Nick Price
were also under par with 69s.

Now my juices are flowing. I haven't felt as positive in a long time.

Tom Watson

Any time you are two shots under par in the U.S. Open, you feel like you're 22 again.
Jack Nicklaus

One minute you're on top of the world and the next you're struggling like little baby turtles coming off the Galapagos Islands.
Mac O'Grady

Mark Twain is said to have written, "I spent the coldest winter of my life one summer in San Francisco." If old Samuel Clemens had been at The Olympic Club on Friday, he probably would have said it again. The fog and clouds remained and the temperature dropped, dipping near 50 degrees by the end of the day.

The players loved it, because the wind was still barely above a whisper, the course stayed soft — relatively — and the greens again were receptive and puttable — relatively.

Tom Watson especially loved it. He is a favorite in San Francisco because he graduated from Stanford University, down the road in Palo Alto, and he was cheered wildly by the gallery as he raced around in 65, five under par and just one shot off the Olympic record of 64 by Rives McBee in 1966.

Off at 8:44 in the morning, Watson arrived at the practice tee early and made an adjustment, shortening and firming the swing that had been giving him trouble for so long. It took a while for the change to work, but in the meantime he lived by his putting stroke, which he had also altered, taking the hands out of play and using his arms and shoulders, as he had done in his heyday. He was hitting

Opposite page, longtime caddy Bruce Edwards helped steer Tom Watson out of his three-year slump.

the putts more solidly and they started falling, beginning with a cup-rattling fifty-footer for birdie on the third hole. "I was lucky," he said. "I hit it too hard. If it had missed the hole it would have gone ten or fifteen feet past."

Watson birdied the ninth with a thirty-footer and the eleventh with a twenty-five-footer. Standing on the fourteenth tee, he felt really comfortable over the ball for the first time. "I just decided to turn it loose," he said, and he ripped the drive well more than 300 yards, leaving only a wedge to the green on the difficult 417-yard par-four. He nipped that shot to within eight feet and made the putt for birdie. On the sixteenth, he hit an eight-iron third shot six feet away and made that putt. A bunkered second shot at the seventeenth cost him his only bogey of the day, but he came back with a four-footer on the eighteenth for his sixth birdie.

"The light switch came on," said Watson, calling it "one of the top ten rounds of my career."

The winner of eight major championships, second behind Nicklaus on the all-time money list with more than $4 million, six times Player of the Year, Watson had been fighting his bewildering slump for almost three years, unable to put a finger on his problem. "It's like climbing uphill in sand," he said.

When asked what winning this Open would mean, he gave the obvious answer. "A lot!" he declared. "Winning this tournament would mean I'm back."

Watson has had the same caddy, Bruce Edwards, for fourteen years, the longest such relationship on Tour, and he credited Edwards for the emergence. "He's made a huge difference," Watson said. "He's been very positive. He kicks me in the rear end to get me going when I'm down.

"Now my juices are flowing. I haven't felt as positive in a long time."

He was now at three under par and the sole

leader of the Open, but that was to last only four hours, until Mark Wiebe brought home an erratic 67 to tie. Once a student at nearby San Jose State, he was authoring a daily column this week for the San Jose *Mercury-News*. Friday he authored one of the championship's more interesting rounds.

Wiebe birdied the first and third holes, followed with three straight bogeys, then birdied the eighth and ninth for an outgoing 34. On the 390-yard twelfth, he struck a 114-yard pitch into the hole for an eagle. Then he bogeyed the thirteenth and birdied the fifteenth.

"I'm mentally tired," he said, which is understandable.

Wiebe, 29, eight years younger than Watson, confessed that when he was in high school he used to stand over putts and say, "This is to beat Tom Watson for the U.S. Open." On Saturday, he was to get that chance for real.

The shared lead was tenuous, however. By day's end, five players were bunched at two under par, a stroke behind.

First came Jim Thorpe, a damaged left thumb deadened by cortisone, his short game sharp because the injury wouldn't let him practice anything else. He shot 68 with a four-birdie, two-bogey round. Thorpe, who admits to being no great shakes as a putter, birdied the eleventh, twelfth and fourteenth on the back nine with putts ranging from eighteen to thirty feet.

Second Round

Tom Watson	65-137
Mark Wiebe	67-137
Jim Thorpe	68-138
Tommy Nakajima	70-138
Jack Nicklaus	68-138
Bernhard Langer	69-138
John Cook	68-138

Next came Tommy Nakajima with one birdie, one bogey and an even-par 70. Nakajima, who outdrove fellow competitors Watson and Hale Irwin on almost every hole, had reported

*Mac O'Grady (left) and Larry Mize were contenders
after sub-par scores in the second round.*

making a change in his game after playing badly in the Masters two months before. But he wouldn't reveal the secret to his new swing for fear it would lose its magic, so the world may forever wonder.

Bernhard Langer, fighting a troublesome driver, recorded his second straight 69 with the use of a lot of irons off the tee.

John Cook, the former Ohio State player who won the U.S. Amateur in 1978 and has spent an up-and-down eight years on Tour, tacked a 68 onto his opening 70 to join the logjam.

Finally there was Ohio State's most famous golfing alumnus. Jack Nicklaus, still struggling but holding on brilliantly, made two thirty-footers at the first and twelfth and a twenty-footer at the sixteenth to offset a three-putt bogey at the fourteenth. His 68 definitely was not a thing of beauty. Having hit only seven fairways Thursday, he got his ball in only eight Friday. He also missed six greens, but he saved par each time with some short-game finesse that has generally not been his strength over the years.

Jack Nicklaus' 68 caused much excitement.

"I'm still not playing well, but I'm scoring very well," Nicklaus said. "The thing that upsets me is that I'm not doing the easy part of the game well. Usually it's the putting that gives you trouble as you get older. It's easy to hit the ball, but I'm not doing that well, and it's driving me batty. I have four or five swing thoughts and I don't know which one to use."

Still, Nicklaus remained Nicklaus. "The game of golf is mind over matter," he declared. "I expect to play well every time I tee it up. I have to believe I can win. I know I'm not as good as I was ten years ago, and I accept that. I can't practice and do the things I used to do. I have to budget my body. But I'm also smarter.

"And any time you are two shots under par in the U.S. Open," Jack said, "you feel like you're 22 again."

But Nicklaus is not 22. He is 47. He had just tied two Open records by competing in his thirty-first consecutive championship and making the cut for the twenty-seventh time, and there was a nagging doubt that the swing or the body, no matter how well-budgeted, could hold up over the next two pressure-filled days.

Ben Crenshaw and Larry Mize, fellow competitors the first two days, went in opposite directions but ended up in a four-man tie at 139, one under par and threatening.

Crenshaw, unable to consistently judge the pace of the greens and not striking the ball solidly, was out in two-over 37, then came home with two birdies and two bogeys to finish at 72 for the round. "It wasn't something to build on," he said.

Mize, after a two-under 68, announced he was happy with his round. He was especially happy with the fifty-seven-yard pitch he holed for birdie on the fifth. "But it wasn't quite the same as Augusta," he grinned.

Also at one under were the veteran Bob Eastwood, back in form after recovering from a shoulder injury incurred last year while wrestling with his teenage son, and Scott Simpson. Eastwood parlayed solid ball-striking and excellent putting into six birdies and a four-under 66. Simpson put together solid nines of 34 each for a 68 that was marred only by a bogey on the long sixteenth. It was the only time in the championship he was to be par or better on the front side, but that was not to be the case on the incoming nine.

Mac O'Grady eagled the first hole Friday to

Mark Wiebe held second place.

start a run of three opening threes, parred the fourth and fifth holes, then made threes on the sixth through the eighth. That gaudy start put him five under par for the round and the Open leader at four under.

"It was going so easy, no labor. The child was ready to be born," said O'Grady, who says things like that.

Then he bogeyed the ninth, double-bogeyed the tenth and bogeyed the twelfth to fall off the leaderboard. Still, he finished with 69 and an even-par 140, undismayed by it all.

"You get the taste of success, you see the filet mignon and reach for the Rothschild wine, and then you see it's Gallo," O'Grady proclaimed. "When you're going, it's as easy as playing junior golf. Then you're mutilated, and it shakes your roots that cling to the earth.

"One minute you're on top of the world and the next you're struggling like little baby turtles coming off the Galapagos Islands."

Okay, Mac.

Above, Tommy Nakajima and, opposite page, Bob Eastwood were also high on the leader boards.

Above, Scott Simpson and, opposite page, Jim Thorpe got in good position with second-round 68s.

O'Grady was one of six at even par. Lennie Clements continued his consistent play with a second straight 70. Lefthander Russ Cochran shot a 69 that was something less than consistent. His first seven holes showed eagle, birdie, bogey, birdie, par, bogey, birdie. "After the fourth hole, it was hard to remember what happened," he said.

Also level for the championship were Craig Stadler with a Friday 68, Jumbo Ozaki, the Japanese bomber, with a 69, and Ed Dougherty, who returned to the Tour this year after a stint as a club professional, who raced in at dusk with a 67.

Six more, including Raymond Floyd (73), Greg Norman (69 after bouncing his tee shot on the 288-yard seventh off a sprinkler head and onto the green), Bob Tway (71), Mark Calcavecchia (68), Tony Sills (70) and Gene Sauers (69 with thirteen consecutive pars from the third through the fifteenth holes) were at 141.

Dale Douglass, after an opening 70, slipped to 73 but became the first reigning U.S. Senior Open champion to make the cut. He was in a gangsome of seventeen at 143.

A record 77 players made the cut, forcing the USGA to send them off in groups of three instead of the usual pairings of two for Saturday's play.

Of the 77, a whole bunch were solidly in the chase. There were fifteen players within three strokes of Watson and Wiebe, twenty-one within four strokes and twenty-eight within five. Add the seventeen at 143, six back, plus the eight more at 144, and a mass melee was in the offing. Given the strength of the course and the difficulty in making up ground on it, players at 145 and above were figured to be out of the running. Or were they?

There were twenty-four rounds below par on Friday, tying the Open record set in the second round at Oakland Hills two years before, and another eleven at par. But with sunny and breezy conditions predicted for Saturday, the course promised to be faster and harder.

The birdie barrage was over.

Apparently no one thought to tell Keith Clearwater.

87th
U. S. Open
Third Round

Starting out, I didn't feel like I was going to shoot 64. . .but then, I never do.
Keith Clearwater

Anybody with a chance to win is nervous. Some deal with it better than others.
Tom Watson

Had it not been for his wife, Keith Clearwater would have been watching this Open on television.

Clearwater is a 28-year-old Californian with classic good looks. With his mustache, now removed, he resembles a slender Clark Gable. Now living in Orem, Utah, he is in his first year on Tour after failing four times in the Qualifying School. In May he had won the rain-delayed National Invitation Tournament at Colonial in Fort Worth, one of the country's toughest courses, by shooting a pair of 64s on Sunday.

Much later that night — about 2:30 the next morning, in fact — Clearwater retired from the interviewing and celebrating and went to bed. He was faced with rising at 5 a.m. to go through 36 holes of local qualifying for the Open, and when that early hour arrived, Keith decided there would be other Opens and prepared to sleep in.

It was then that his wife, Sue, set the record straight. "Get up and get out there," she said. "A week from now you'll wish you had." A nudge in the back with a pair of feet sealed that decision. Clearwater got through the local rounds, then the sectional qualifying to make it to the main event.

After a 74 start on Thursday at Olympic — "a very poor ball-striking round," he said later

Opposite page, Keith Clearwater started early and saw his record-equalling 64 become even more impressive as the third day wore on.

— Clearwater came back with a 71 in the second round. At 145, tied for fifty-sixth place and eight shots behind Tom Watson and Mark Wiebe, he didn't figure to be a threat.

Off at 8:30 Saturday morning and just trying to play himself into position, Clearwater simply annihilated the proud Lake Course with a six-birdie, no-bogey round of 64. That tied a 21-year-old competitive course record set by Rives McBee, an unknown club professional from Texas, in the second round of the 1966 Open at Olympic. It also tied Ben Crenshaw's Open record for the third round, set at Merion in 1981.

Clearwater's shocking score, over a course that was to yield only nine other sub-par rounds on the day, put him not only in position but solidly in contention. For a long time during the ensuing hours, as Watson struggled and others fell away, he even held a share of the lead.

Clearwater missed only four greens, three on the fringe and once in a bunker, and saved par each time. He birdied the difficult fourth with a six-foot putt, the eighth with a ten-footer, the ninth from six inches, the eleventh from twenty feet, the sixteenth from twelve feet and the seventeenth from eight. He required just twenty-six putts on greens that had been giving the field fits all week.

"I played very conservatively tee to green and putted well," said Clearwater, in something of an understatement. "You just try to maintain yourself all the way around. Just keep the ball in play and be really patient. Starting out, I didn't feel like I was going to shoot 64. . . .but then, I never do."

Clearwater finished just after the leaders started. By this time, the early fog was burning off and the sun was peeking through occasionally. Eventually it would shine at full force, speeding and firming the greens and making them susceptible to spike marks.

For awhile, it looked as if Clearwater would be the leader by default. While Watson and Wiebe, who started at three under, were playing the first hole, Jack Nicklaus and Bernhard Langer both birdied it to pull into a four-way tie. But Open pressure, or the gods of Olympic, soon began to nibble away at the contenders.

Third Round

Tom Watson	71-208
Keith Clearwater	64-209
Scott Simpson	70-209
Lennie Clements	70-210
John Mahaffey	67-211
Seve Ballesteros	68-211
Larry Mize	72-211
Ben Crenshaw	72-211
Bernhard Langer	73-211
Jim Thorpe	73-211

Watson and Wiebe both bogeyed the first hole, Tom with three putts from thirty feet.

Nicklaus bogeyed the second, leaving Langer the sole leader. The German immediately came to grief with bogey on the 223-yard third hole.

When Lennie Clements, after a 70-70 start to the championship, birdied the first and fourth holes, he joined Watson, Wiebe, Nicklaus, Langer, Tommy Nakajima and Larry Mize in a seven-way tie for the lead. But the attrition continued.

Watson bogeyed the third, three-putting from the front fringe, and the fourth when he put his second over the green and missed a twelve-footer for par. He was now level for the championship, his putter faltering and his comeback dream fading.

Nicklaus and Langer both bogeyed the fifth. Clements, who had bogeyed the sixth but birdied the seventh, and Wiebe now were tied at two under par. Legions were within hailing distance.

Jim Thorpe, starting at two under par in the last group, bogeyed the first two holes and

*Tom Watson's 71-208 left him one stroke in front of Clearwater
and, opposite page, Scott Simpson.*

triple-bogeyed the fifth to go five over par for the round.

Up ahead, despite a pollen reaction that was causing sneezes and red eyes, Seve Ballesteros was making noises. Playing aggressively, hitting only drivers off the tee, he was out in 33 with two bogeys and four birdies. He birdied the eleventh and thirteenth to go one under for the championship, slipped with a bogey at the fourteenth, then regained the stroke with a birdie at the fifteenth. Bogeys at the long sixteenth and the finishing hole would slow his charge and put him in at 68, one over for the three rounds but clearly challenging.

Wiebe holed a curling fourteen-footer at the fifth to become the sole leader at three under. Langer birdied the sixth to join Clements in second place at two under. Ben Crenshaw, hanging in at even par through his first eight holes, was another stroke back, tied with Nicklaus and Clearwater.

Mize had double-bogeyed the seventh, which was to become a pivotal hole, to drop to one over par, where he was to finish.

Wiebe parred the sixth and looked to be under control going to the 288-yard seventh with its diabolical three-tiered green. Up ahead, both Langer and Nicklaus had failed to get their second shots back to the hole on the top level, and both three-putted from mid-green.

Wiebe drove well, but his ball lodged in a divot in the fairway. He hit his second shot heavy and got the ball only to the first level of the green, miles from the cup, from where he three-putted. Not until late Sunday afternoon would any player again be as much as three under standard figures.

Watson, meanwhile, had been talking to himself. "I felt very calm," he said. "The wheels hadn't fallen off. I told myself to hang in there."

Watson then punched his second shot on the seventh to the top level, ten feet away, and holed the putt — one under again.

Wiebe's tee shot on the tiny eighth caught the tree overhanging the right side and dropped into a bunker. Bogey. Clements, a 30-year-old from San Diego who had never won in six and a half years on Tour, saved par with a fifteen-foot putt on the eleventh and was in the lead by himself.

Not for long. Clements bogeyed the twelfth and fell into a tie with Watson, Wiebe, Crenshaw — who was through eleven holes — and Keith Clearwater, now bashing balls on the

The Olympic Club provided excellent viewing areas for the sellout crowds.

practice tee. Clearwater was to remain in that position for the next hour and a half.

Watson and Wiebe both parred the ninth, Watson with a marvelous shot from heavy rough behind the green. The field was now on the back nine and the sun was breaking through.

Scott Simpson was in the middle of what he later called "a strange round." For the first six holes he found neither a fairway nor a green in regulation, bogeying the second, fifth and sixth holes and falling back to two over par. Then he "made a little change" and hit the last twelve greens. When he lashed a six-iron to eight feet on the ninth and made the putt for birdie, he was back to one over par.

Wiebe's demise accelerated on the tenth hole. He drove left into an unplayable lie and, after his drop, saved bogey with a brilliant shot from the trees, but his time had passed. He bogeyed the twelfth after bunkering his second shot. He chili-dipped his second shot on the par-three thirteenth, then holed his third for par. Then he vanished, bogeying the fifteenth, seventeenth and eighteenth holes and finishing with 77, four over par for the championship. His 79 on Sunday left him near the bottom of the standings.

Nicklaus was traveling the same road. He was reverting to his new putting ways, missing the putts he had made in the past — a five-footer for par on the tenth, a four-footer for par on the par-three thirteenth after a wonderful pitch shot from the left rough. He bogeyed the sixteenth and seventeenth on the way home for a round of 76 that put him out of the running.

Crenshaw also drove to the left on the thirteenth and bogeyed, then followed with a bogey on the fourteenth. He parred in to finish at two-over 72, one over for the championship, and promptly declared, "I aged five years today."

Nakajima stroked a ten-foot putt for birdie on the tenth that he obviously thought he had missed. When instead it toppled in, he was again one under and tied for the lead.

Clements bogeyed the short fifteenth when he bunkered his tee shot, but he recovered with a thirty-foot chip-in for birdie on the sixteenth.

Heading into the closing holes, then, it was

Seve Ballesteros charged back to within three strokes of the lead with a third-round 68.

Isao Aoki was in the running at 214.

Watson, Nakajima, Clements and, of course, Clearwater, tied at one under. Langer, holding steady over the back nine, was even. So was Simpson, who struck a seven-iron to eight feet and made birdie on the short fifteenth.

Clements bogeyed the seventeenth to fall back to even, where he finished after parring the eighteenth for his third straight 70. Shortly thereafter, Nakajima birdied the fifteenth from twenty feet to take an undisputed but short-lived lead.

Watson, making steady two-putt pars on the back nine, struck an eight-iron to fifteen feet at the fifteenth and holed for a birdie. At the same time, Nakajima bunkered his third shot at the sixteenth and bogeyed. Watson, for the first time since the opening hole, was the sole leader at two under.

Nakajima took an adventurous route home. He drove well to the right on the seventeenth and his ball ended atop a spectator's sweatshirt. That's a movable obstruction and

Countryman Tommy Nakajima offered a strong challenge until losing a ball in a tree on the eighteenth hole.

Tommy was allowed a free drop. It didn't help, because he left his next shot short and failed to make par.

On the eighteenth, Nakajima drove into the right rough, then pushed his second shot into a large pine to the right of the fairway. The tree proved to be a less forgiving obstacle, swallowing the ball. A young spectator climbed the tree in a fruitless search, and Nakajima was forced to declare the ball lost. After another drop, he made a depressing double-bogey for a round of 74 and never really recovered.

While Nakajima was undergoing his travail, Simpson was making a ten-foot putt for birdie on the eighteenth for an incoming 33 and a 70 to return to one under par for the three rounds.

Playing the best golf of his life prior to the Open, Simpson was in contention.

When Watson took three putts to negotiate sixty feet from the back fringe on the seventeenth, he was tied for the lead with Simpson

and Clearwater, now watching the action from his hotel room.

Watson quickly broke the deadlock. On the eighteenth, he lofted a nine-iron 115 yards from the middle of the fairway to fifteen feet, slightly above and to the right of the hole. It was a dangerous putt that broke at least four feet. But Watson read it perfectly and the ball fell in the top side, giving him a round of 71 and a two-under-par total. A "no-brainer," Tom said afterward.

Huck Finn was back on top in the quest for his second U.S. Open title. But about half the golfing world was on his heels.

"I'll be very nervous, obviously," Watson said. "I'm going to play a round of golf tomorrow that will be one of the most important in my career. I know that and you know that.

"Anybody with a chance to win is nervous. Some deal with it better than others."

Then he said, "In the U.S. Open, there's more courage involved in playing the last round than in any other tournament."

 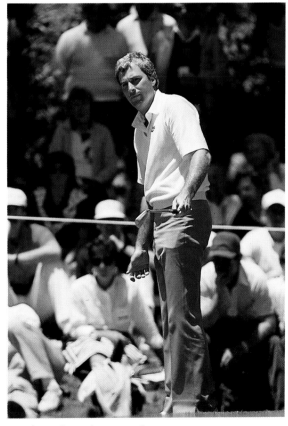

*Dan Pohl (left) and Curtis Strange kept their championship
hopes alive with 69s.*

I can't believe you can play this well with the conditions on this golf course.

Jack Nicklaus

He hit the shots he had to hit.

Tom Watson

I've always wondered if I'd be good enough to win something like this. This is incredible. It's a dream come true, and it will take a long time to sink in.

Scott Simpson

Tom Watson, the veteran, was admittedly nervous. Keith Clearwater, the new kid on the block, was outwardly relaxed. Scott Simpson was being ignored.

The Olympic Club's Lake Course was ready, its bite restored. P.J. Boatwright, Jr., the USGA's Executive Director, Rules and Competitions, proclaimed the course to be in "near-perfect" condition. The weather pattern had held — fog shrouded the early starters, but by mid-morning there was barely a cloud in the sky and the temperatures were heading for the high sixties.

Most U.S. Opens are lost, not won, as challengers dissolve in the molten fire of Sunday's pressure. This championship was going to be won, although it didn't look like it at the start.

For much of the round it was Saturday again, almost eerily so in the beginning. Mac O'Grady eagled the first hole to go to even par. Seve Ballesteros and Bernhard Langer birdied the first and were even par for the championship. Lennie Clements parred and stayed even. And Simpson sank from twenty-five feet for birdie to go two under. The field was bunching.

Clearwater rushed his swing off the first

Scott Simpson hits to the scenic final green on his championship march.

tee and pushed his drive far into the trees on the right. He eventually managed a scrambling par, but the pattern had been set.

As he had Saturday, Watson hooked his second into the rough left of the green and eventually three-putted for a bogey. Simpson, who saved par at the second with a ten-foot putt, was in the lead.

Watson was victimized on the second when a well-played second shot bounced over the green and he bogeyed. So did Clearwater, and Simpson momentarily led by two, with Langer, Larry Mize and Mac O'Grady joining Watson and Clearwater at even par.

But Simpson bogeyed the third and fourth holes, missing from six feet and twenty-five feet. At that point he was even par, tied for the lead with Watson, who had saved par from the bunker on the third with a five-foot putt, and Mize, who had done the same on the fifth hole.

As Simpson was making a two-putt par at the fifth, Langer was missing from six feet for birdie on the seventh and Mize was missing his par from three feet on the sixth. Watson promptly three-putted the fifth and Simpson again was alone on top.

Clearwater, who had bogeyed the second and double-bogeyed the third, hooked his tee shot into the rough on the fifth, made bogey and was sinking fast on his way to 79, fifteen strokes higher than his Saturday round.

Simpson bogeyed the sixth and now was tied for the lead at one over with Watson, Langer, Mize and O'Grady, who was through the twelfth. Curtis Strange, out in 35, Ben Crenshaw, through seven, and Tommy Nakajima, through twelve, all lurked at two over, with Ballesteros, John Mahaffey, Clements, Clearwater, Bobby Wadkins, Jim Thorpe and Tim Simpson another stroke away. Nobody, at this point, seemed destined to win the trophy. So far, the course was the clear winner.

That was to change. Neither Scott Simpson nor Tom Watson were to make another bogey in this championship.

On the short par-four seventh, Simpson's pitch just hung on the edge of the second level, ten feet from where the hole was cut, and he made the putt for birdie and the outright lead.

Ballesteros was making a move with birdies on the seventh and eighth and now was just a stroke back at one over.

Crenshaw birdied the ninth from ten feet. Now he was tied with Ballesteros, Watson, Langer, Mize and O'Grady for second.

Watson chipped nicely out of the rough fronting the seventh green to eight feet, but he missed the birdie. Then he struck a nine-iron fifteen feet away on the eighth and rolled that in. The championship was tied again, and moments later Mize and Crenshaw both made short putts to birdie the tenth and make it a foursome at the top.

After Simpson parred the ninth and tenth, Watson hit a pitching wedge on the 433-yard ninth to fifteen feet and made it for birdie to take the lead. His eight-iron second on the tenth finished ten feet away, but the birdie putt spun out of the cup. He smiled grimly, the nervousness gone. The old magic was coming back, and Tom Watson was twenty-two again and charging.

Crenshaw and Mize both bogeyed the twelfth hole while Ballesteros was making birdie on the eleventh to move to even par.

Periscopes were often essential to view the front-runners.

Simpson got a wonderful break on the eleventh after pushing his second shot into the lefthand bunker. He hit his sand shot thin and the ball was headed for the far edge of the green. But it caught the flag on the way down and spun back to within two feet of the cup, from where Simpson tapped in for his par. Still even.

The challengers now were ebbing and flowing, Ballesteros, Langer and Crenshaw bouncing between one over and two over and back to one. Mize was fading away. O'Grady and Nakajima both bogeyed the sixteenth and seventeenth to go four over and out of it.

Simpson saved par on the twelfth with a pitch and a short putt, just as Watson did moments later. He two-putted the thirteenth from sixty feet for par, and Watson, short with a six-iron on the same 186-yard hole, saved his par with an excellent pitch from a bad lie.

Simpson drove perfectly on the 417-yard fourteenth and put a seven-iron four feet from the hole. Birdie. One under and tied. Suddenly, all those floating around over par were of no account. Scott Simpson was about to take charge of the U.S. Open.

On the fifteenth, the heavily bunkered little par-three, Simpson hit a nine-iron thirty feet short and below the hole and rolled in the putt. Birdie, two under and the lead, momentarily.

Watson had driven in the left rough on the fourteenth and hit a pitching wedge to the top

Tom Watson (left) opened the way with a poor start,
then could not hold off steady Scott Simpson.

of the green, twenty feet away. When he heard the roar from the fifteenth, he knew the game was on. He responded by trickling his putt into the side of the cup. Tied again.

On the long sixteenth, Simpson pushed his tee shot into the trees on the right. But Simpson's ball ended up in a relatively clean lie where the gallery had trampled the grass, and he drilled a perfect two-iron shot under the trees to the middle of the fairway.

Watson put a nine-iron on the fifteenth green forty feet short, putted to within five feet, then made the tester, the ball circling the lip before it fell in.

Simpson, playing from the right side of the fairway to a hole cut on the right side of the green and guarded by a gaping bunker, selected a nine-iron. The shot flew directly at the flag, landed barely over the bunker in the heavy rough, a foot from disaster, and bounced onto the green, fifteen feet past the cup.

Watson drove perfectly and long down the right side of the sixteenth and struck a two-iron down the heart of the narrow fairway, leaving his ball 100 yards from the hole.

Then he stood and watched while Simpson stroked his birdie putt into the cup.

Jack Nicklaus, now turned television commentator after finishing with 77 and 291, said from the eighteenth tower, "I can't believe you can play this well with the conditions on this golf course."

Watson burned a sand wedge directly at the flag and checked it up fifteen feet beyond. The fans sitting behind the sixteenth green all day knew the putt did not break to the right. Nicklaus, on television, said it did not break. Watson later said he pulled the putt. Whatever. He missed by three inches on the left.

Up ahead, on the seventeenth, Simpson's drive slipped into the first cut of rough on the right. Then he pulled a four-iron into the left front bunker and faced a treacherous thirty-yard downhill shot with the ball resting below his feet in the sand. A tie loomed.

*Mac O'Grady (left) and Larry Mize were among
the many final-round contenders.*

Simpson then saved the Open, playing a superb shot that landed barely on the green and trickled to a stop six feet below the cup. Then he made the putt, climaxing an amazing four-hole run and, in his own words, the best putting day of his life.

Watson, again with a perfect drive that even stayed in the fairway, whacked a five-iron forty-feet beyond and to the left of the cup and managed a perilous two-putt for par.

Simpson, who had looked at the leaderboard for the first time as he left the sixteenth green, nervelessly put a two-iron down the middle of the eighteenth fairway. From 127 yards, he swung an eight-iron smoothly and stopped the ball twenty feet below the hole. Two putts later he had a round of 68, a total of 277 and the championship — almost.

Watson still had the eighteenth to play. Again he drove flawlessly with a two iron. From 113 yards, he chose a pitching wedge for his second, and that was a mistake. "It was probably a nine-iron," he said. "I thought the

In addition to Watson and Mize, there were three other Masters winners in the chase: Bernhard Langer (top right), Seve Ballesteros (above left) and Ben Crenshaw (above right).

Tom Watson's desperation birdie try was an inch or so shy of the hole at the eighteenth, leaving him to be consoled by caddy Bruce Edwards (inset).

wind was with me, but after I hit the shot I took two steps and felt it in my face."

Fourth Round

Scott Simpson	68-277
Tom Watson	70-278
Seve Ballesteros	71-282
Bobby Wadkins	71-283
Curtis Strange	71-283
Bernhard Langer	72-283
Ben Crenshaw	72-283
Larry Mize	72-283

The ball landed well short of the hole and sucked back off onto the front fringe, some thirty-five feet away and against the tall collar.

Watson watched Clearwater putt up the steep slope from nearly the same position. "It's the hardest you have to hit a putt on the golf course," he said. "I knew I'd have to rip it."

Rip it he did, gallantly. The ball started to bounce but stayed on line. . . .and drifted to a stop just three inches short.

Bitterly disappointed and near tears after-ward, Watson still knew that he had not lost the Open. Simpson had won it.

"Scott Simpson is a very fine golfer," Watson said. "This doesn't surprise me. He hit the shots he had to hit.

"I have nothing to be ashamed of. I hit good shots today, and I'm proud of the way I played. I didn't keep the mistakes from happening with the putter, but I played well enough to win."

Second is not good enough, of course, for Tom Watson, who must win if only to prove something to himself. But now he thinks he can.

"There's a lot of golf left in Tom Watson," he said. "A lot."

Simpson's reaction was almost bewilderment.

"I've always wondered if I'd be good enough to win something like this," he said. "This is incredible. It's a dream come true, and it will take a long time to sink in."

On this day, when he had the opportunity, he was good enough, and the wonderment is that he wondered. After all, he said early on that Scott Simpson could win the Open.

Scott Simpson's crucial shots down the stretch included his bunker shot (opposite page) and six-foot par putt on the seventeenth, his birdie putt on the sixteenth (above left) and a clinching par at the eighteenth (above right).

The strength of my game is consistency, and that's what you need at Olympic.
Scott Simpson

The Hard Rock Cafe on Van Ness Street in San Francisco is a former automobile showroom converted into a huge food, drink and rock music emporium that caters to the young, fun-loving crowd. It would be an unlikely place to find a quiet, devout man of thirty-one who was about to win the United States Open.

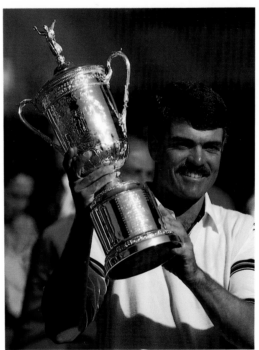

But the Hard Rock makes good hamburgers, and Scott Simpson loves hamburgers. So on Saturday night, just hours before he was to trample Tom Watson and everybody else on the way to golf's most prestigious championship, Simpson and his wife, Cheryl, sat in the Hard Rock, he munching on hamburger, she on ribs. And they discussed what would happen should he win the next day. The consensus: not much.

"He thought he had a chance to win," said Cheryl after the smoke had cleared Sunday and Simpson had indeed done just that. "He said if he did, it wouldn't change him, and it won't."

Scott himself was saying that the Open championship might not be as important to him as to other players. God, he said, comes first with him, followed by his wife and two children and then golf, which is never as important as the other two.

But that does not at all mean winning this eighty-seventh U.S. Open title was not important to him. "I feel overwhelmed that I could win a tournament like this," he said. "It's a dream come true. If I could pick one tournament to win, it would be the U.S. Open."

The victory and $150,000 prize raised his 1987 winnings to $465,896, and boosted his career earnings to almost $1.7 million in eight and a half seasons.

The point is, Scott Simpson did not arrive at The Olympic Club from outer space. As he walked off the seventy-second green, the trophy virtually in his grasp, heads were nodding and tongues were wagging — yes, it was the same old story at Olympic, where Ben Hogan lost to an unknown and Arnold Palmer lost to a lesser player. Now the same thing had happened to Watson.

At least half of the Olympic legend is hogwash, of course. While the occasional Jack Fleck does appear from nowhere to win the Open, seldom to be seen again, Billy Casper had already won an Open when he beat Palmer, and he was to wind up in the Hall of Fame. That may or may not happen to Simpson, but the fact is that seventeen different players have won the last seventeen major championships played in the world. That means that an awful lot of people are capable these days, and Scott Simpson is certainly one of them. After his rookie season in 1979, he has never finished worse than forty-first on the PGA Tour money list. He had won three tournaments prior to the Open, all on difficult courses. He's a solid player, respected by his peers, who know.

"That wasn't just good golf those guys played," Jack Nicklaus said afterwards. "It was sensational golf."

Simpson played the incoming nine in 32 strokes, the last twelve holes four under par in a ferocious stretch of golf. "If I ever played better, I can't remember it," he said.

Neither he nor Watson wavered under the pressure. Simpson just made more putts. He used only twenty-six putts all day, one-putting six times on the back nine. But that's part of the game, too, usually the part affected first by shaky nerves.

"Scott doesn't get nervous at all," said Cheryl with a smile. "He's really calm, really a laid-back person."

Staying calm has been easier since he accepted Christianity three years ago. "That was a personal decision and I hope it doesn't turn people off," he said, "but it's the most important thing in my life."

Simpson used to have a lot of trouble staying cool. He is a San Diego native who has been playing golf in California for years, and one San Francisco columnist says, "As an amateur, he was the biggest hothead I ever saw."

Simpson blames the temper on inheritance. He got it from his father, Joe, a trumpet player in a San Diego society band and a two-handicap golfer. What he also got recently was some fatherly encouragement that helped him win the Open.

"Dad and I played here a few weeks ago, and he said I could win here, that this course was made for me," Simpson recalled. "Here you have to drive the ball straight, hit good irons and be good around the greens. The strength of my game is consistency, and that's what you need at Olympic."

Consistency. Fairways and greens, just plodding along. Jack Nicklaus said a plodder would win, remember?

Simpson, who was introduced to golf at the age of nine when he started caddying for his father, has been plodding along for years, although at a higher level than most of us.

A 1978 graduate of the University of Southern California with a degree in business administration, he had a distinguished, if unheralded, amateur career.

He won the Pacific Eight individual championship in 1975 and 1977, the NCAA title in 1976 and 1977 and the Porter Cup in 1976. He was a member of the 1977 Walker Cup team.

Still, he failed twice to make it through the Tour Qualifying School, finally getting his card in the fall of 1978. He won the 1980 Western Open over the treacherous Butler National course, then waited four years before winning at Westchester in 1984.

This spring, two weeks before the Masters, he won the Greater Greensboro Open on a strong Forest Oaks Country Club layout.

The reason that 1987 became his best season ever was that he gave up trying to get better.

"In 1985 I decided that I needed to change my game, that I had to hit the ball farther," he said. "So I worked on that in 1985 and 1986. I went to three or four different teachers. But for me to change was difficult. At the end of 1986 I took eleven weeks off and reflected on where I wanted to go. I decided to go back to my own game. I forgot everything my teachers had been telling me, and I've been playing a lot better."

Simpson is a Hogan disciple, although he does not try to swing like Hogan. "I just try to keep a good center and make a good turn, Hogan's fundamentals," he said. "And I try to think like him, to discipline myself like he did."

And now, ironically, Simpson has accomplished at The Olympic Club what Hogan was unable to do.

Although he hides it well, as any laid-back Southern Californian would do, Simpson has a sense of humor, sometimes on the wry side. Several years ago, past Western Open champions were gathered at a dinner celebrating the tournament's seventy-fifth anniversary. Each spoke briefly, or not so briefly, on what winning the Western had meant.

Simpson's speech was by far the briefest. "I just want to say that the Western Open victory has been the most important of my career," he told the audience. "That's because it's my only one."

Now he has some others, including the biggest one of all.

87th U. S. Open

Statistics

Hole	1	2	3	4	5	6	7	8	9	10	11	12	13	14	15	16	17	18	Total
Par	5	4	3	4	4	4	4	3	4	4	4	4	3	4	3	5	4	4	70

Scott Simpson

	1	2	3	4	5	6	7	8	9	10	11	12	13	14	15	16	17	18	Total	
Round 1	6	4	3	4	4	4	4	2	4	4	4	4	3	5	2	5	5	4	71	
Round 2	5	4	3	4	4	4	4	2	4	4	4	3	3	4	2	6	4	4	68	
Round 3	5	5	3	4	5	5	4	3	3	4	4	4	3	4	2	5	4	3	70	
Round 4	4	4	4	5	4	5	3	3	4	4	4	4	3	3	2	4	4	4	68	277

Tom Watson

	1	2	3	4	5	6	7	8	9	10	11	12	13	14	15	16	17	18	Total	
Round 1	4	6	2	4	4	4	4	4	4	4	4	5	3	4	3	6	3	4	72	
Round 2	5	4	2	4	4	4	4	3	3	4	3	4	3	3	3	4	5	3	65	
Round 3	6	4	4	5	4	4	3	3	4	4	4	4	3	4	2	5	5	3	71	
Round 4	6	5	3	4	5	4	4	2	3	4	4	4	3	3	3	5	4	4	70	278

Seve Ballesteros

	1	2	3	4	5	6	7	8	9	10	11	12	13	14	15	16	17	18	Total	
Round 1	5	4	3	4	4	4	4	3	4	3	4	3	2	4	3	6	4	4	68	
Round 2	5	4	3	4	5	4	5	3	5	4	4	5	3	4	4	5	4	4	75	
Round 3	4	5	3	3	3	3	4	4	4	4	3	4	2	5	2	6	4	5	68	
Round 4	4	4	4	5	5	4	3	2	4	4	3	5	4	4	2	5	5	4	71	282

Hole	Par	Eagles	Birdies	Pars	Bogeys	Higher	Rank	Average
1	5	7	110	256	85	7	18	4.95
2	4	0	37	264	135	29	4	4.34
3	3	0	41	273	138	13	5	3.26
4	4	0	22	279	148	16	3	4.35
5	4	0	22	247	171	24	2	4.43
6	4	0	53	265	128	18	8	4.24
7	4	1	91	289	74	9	16	4.00
8	3	0	74	315	64	10	15	3.03
9	4	1	54	286	98	24	9	4.20
OUT	35	9	504	2474	1041	150		36.80
10	4	0	52	305	95	11	11	4.14
11	4	0	43	278	123	19	5	4.26
12	4	1	62	299	92	9	13	4.10
13	3	0	50	307	99	7	11	3.14
14	4	0	56	281	109	17	10	4.19
15	3	0	87	302	66	8	17	2.99
16	5	0	58	250	137	18	7	5.25
17	4	0	17	213	199	34	1	4.56
18	4	0	64	297	94	8	13	4.10
IN	35	1	489	2532	1014	131		36.73
TOTAL	70	10	993	5006	2055	281		73.53

ate	Winner, Runner-Up	Score	Site	Entry
·95 (Oct.)	**Horace Rawlins** Willie Dunn	173 175	**Newport G.C.,** Newport, R.I.	11
·96 (July)	**James Foulis** Horace Rawlins	†152 155	**Shinnecock Hills G.C.,** Southampton, N.Y.	35
·97 (Sept.)	**Joe Lloyd** Willie Anderson	162 163	**Chicago G.C.,** Wheaton, Ill.	35
·98 (June)	**Fred Herd** Alex Smith	328 335	**Myopia Hunt Club,** S. Hamilton, Mass.	49
·99 (Sept.)	**Willie Smith** George Low/Val Fitzjohn/W.H. Way	315 326	**Baltimore C.C.,** (Roland Park Course) Baltimore, Md.	81
·00 (Oct.)	**Harry Vardon** J.H. Taylor	313 315	**Chicago G.C.,** Wheaton, Ill.	60
·01 (June)	**Willie Anderson** Alex Smith	331-85 331-86	**Myopia Hunt Club,** S. Hamilton, Mass.	60
·02 (Oct.)	**Lawrence Auchterlonie** Stewart Gardner/*Walter J. Travis	307 313	**Garden City, G.C.** Garden City, N.Y.	90
·03 (June)	**Willie Anderson** David Brown	307-82 307-84	**Baltusrol G.C.,** (original course) Springfield, N.J.	89
·04 (July)	**Willie Anderson** Gilbert Nicholls	303 308	**Glen View Club,** Golf, Ill.	71
·05 (Sept.)	**Willie Anderson** Alex Smith	314 316	**Myopia Hunt Club,** S. Hamilton, Mass.	83
·06 (June)	**Alex Smith** William Smith	295 302	**Onwentsia Club,** Lake Forest, Ill.	68
·07 (June)	**Alex Ross** Gilbert Nicholls	302 304	**Philadelphia Cricket C.,** (St. Martins Course) Philadelphia, Pa.	82
·08 (Aug.)	**Fred McLeod** Willie Smith	322-77 322-83	**Myopia Hunt Club,** S. Hamilton, Mass.	88
·09 (June)	**George Sargent** Tom McNamara	290 294	**Englewood G.C.,** Englewood, N.Y.	84
·10 (June)	**Alex Smith** John J. McDermott Macdonald Smith	298-71 298-75 298-77	**Philadelphia Cricket C.,** (St. Martins Course) Philadelphia, Pa.	75
·11 (June)	**John J. McDermott** Michael J. Brady George O. Simpson	307-80 307-82 307-85	**Chicago G.C.,** Wheaton, Ill.	79
·12 (Aug.)	**John J. McDermott** Tom McNamara	294 296	**C.C. of Buffalo,** Buffalo, N.Y.	131
·13 (Sept.)	***Francis Ouimet** Harry Vardon Edward Ray	304-72 304-77 304-78	**The Country Club,** Brookline, Mass.	165
·14 (Aug.)	**Walter Hagen** *Charles Evans, Jr.	290 291	**Midlothian C.C.,** Blue Island, Ill.	129
·15 (June)	***Jerome D. Travers** Tom McNamara	297 298	**Baltusrol G.C.,** (original course) Springfield, N.J.	141
·16 (June)	***Charles Evans, Jr.** Jock Hutchison	286 288	**Minikahda Club,** Minneapolis, Minn.	94
·17-18 — No Championships: World War I				
·19 (June)	**Walter Hagen** Michael J. Brady	301-77 301-78	**Brae Burn C.C.,** West Newton, Mass.	142
·20 (Aug.)	**Edward Ray** Harry Vardon/Jack Burke, Sr./Leo Diegel/Jock Hutchison	295 296	**Inverness Club,** Toledo, Ohio	265
·21 (July)	**James M. Barnes** Walter Hagen/Fred McLeod	289 298	**Columbia C.C.** Chevy Chase, Md.	262
·22 (July)	**Gene Sarazen** *Robert T. Jones, Jr./John L. Black	288 289	**Skokie C.C.,** Glencoe, Ill.	323
·23 (July)	***Robert T. Jones, Jr.** Bobby Cruickshank	296-76 296-78	**Inwood C.C.,** Inwood, N.Y.	360
·24 (June)	**Cyril Walker** *Robert T. Jones, Jr.	297 300	**Oakland Hills C.C.,** (South Course) Birmingham, Mich.	319

Date	Winner, Runner-Up	Score	Site	Ent
1925 (June)	**William Macfarlane** *Robert T. Jones, Jr.	291-75-72 291-75-73	**Worcester C.C.,** Worcester, Mass.	4
1926 (June)	***Robert T. Jones, Jr.** Joe Turnesa	293 294	**Scioto C.C.,** Columbus, Ohio	6
1927 (June)	**Tommy Armour** Harry Cooper	301-76 301-79	**Oakmont C.C.,** Oakmont, Pa.	8
1928 (June)	**Johnny Farrell** *Robert T. Jones, Jr.	294-143 294-144	**Olympia Fields C.C.,** (No. 4 Course) Mateson, Ill.	1,0
1929 (June)	***Robert T. Jones, Jr.** Al Espinosa	294-141 294-164	**Winged Foot G.C.,** (West Course) Mamaroneck, N.Y.	1,0
1930 (July)	***Robert T. Jones, Jr.** Macdonald Smith	287 289	**Interlachen C.C.,** Minneapolis, Minn.	1,1
1931 (July)	**Billy Burke** George Von Elm	292-149-148 292-149-149	**Inverness Club,** Toledo, Ohio	1,1
1932 (June)	**Gene Sarazen** Bobby Cruickshank/T. Philip Perkins	286 289	**Fresh Meadow C.C.,** Flushing, N.Y.	1,0
1933 (June)	***John Goodman** Ralph Guldahl	287 288	**North Shore C.C.,** Glenview, Ill.	9
1934 (June)	**Olin Dutra** Gene Sarazen	293 294	**Merion Cricket C.,** (East Course) Ardmore, Pa.	1,0
1935 (June)	**Sam Parks, Jr.** Jimmy Thomson	299 301	**Oakmont C.C.,** Oakmont, Pa.	1,1
1936 (June)	**Tony Manero** Harry Cooper	282 284	**Baltusrol G.C.,** (Upper Course) Springfield, N.Y.	1,2
1937 (June)	**Ralph Guldahl** Sam Snead	281 283	**Oakland Hills C.C.,** (South Course) Birmingham, Mich.	1,4
1938 (June)	**Ralph Guldahl** Dick Metz	284 290	**Cherry Hills C.C.,** Englewood, Colo.	1,2
1939 (June)	**Byron Nelson** Craig Wood Denny Shute	284-68-70 284-68-73 284-76	**Philadelphia C.C.,** (Spring Mill Course) West Conshohocken, Pa.	1,1
1940 (June)	**Lawson Little** Gene Sarazen	287-70 287-73	**Canterbury, G.C.,** Cleveland, Ohio	1,1
1941 (June)	**Craig Wood** Denny Shute	284 287	**Colonial Club,** Fort Worth, Tex.	1,0
1942-45 — No Championships: World War II				
1946 (June)	**Lloyd Mangrum** Byron Nelson/Victor Ghezzi	284-72-72 284-72-73	**Canterbury, G.C.,** Cleveland, Ohio	1,1
1947 (June)	**Lew Worsham** Sam Snead	282-69 282-70	**St. Louis C.C.,** Clayton, Mo.	1,3
1948 (June)	**Ben Hogan** Jimmy Demaret	276 278	**Riviera C.C.,** Los Angeles, Calif.	1,4
1949 (June)	**Cary Middlecoff** Sam Snead/Clayton Heafner	286 287	**Medinah C.C.,** (No. 3 Course) Medinah, Ill.	1,3
1950 (June)	**Ben Hogan** Lloyd Mangrum George Fazio	287-69 287-73 287-75	**Merion G.C.,** (East Course) Ardmore, Pa.	1,3
1951 (June)	**Ben Hogan** Clayton Heafner	287 289	**Oakland Hills C.C.,** (South Course) Birmingham, Mich.	1,5
1952 (June)	**Julius Boros** Ed (Porky) Oliver	281 285	**Northwood Club,** Dallas, Tex.	1,6
1953 (June)	**Ben Hogan** Sam Snead	283 289	**Oakmont, C.C.,** Oakmont, Pa.	1,6
1954 (June)	**Ed Furgol** Gene Littler	284 285	**Baltusrol G.C.,** (Lower Course) Springfield, N.J.	1,9
1955 (June)	**Jack Fleck** Ben Hogan	287-69 287-72	**Olympic Club,** (Lake Course) San Francisco, Calif.	1,5
1956 (June)	**Cary Middlecoff** Julius Boros/Ben Hogan	281 282	**Oak Hill C.C.,** (East Course) Rochester, N.Y.	1,9
1957 (June)	**Dick Mayer** Cary Middlecoff	282-72 282-79	**Inverness Club,** Toledo, Ohio	1,9
1958 (June)	**Tommy Bolt** Gary Player	283 287	**Southern Hills C.C.,** Tulsa, Okla.	2,1
1959 (June)	**Bill Casper, Jr.** Bob Rosburg	282 283	**Winged Foot G.C.,** (West Course) Mamaroneck, N.Y.	2,3
1960 (June)	**Arnold Palmer** *Jack Nicklaus	280 282	**Cherry Hills C.C.,** Englewood, Colo.	2,4
1961 (June)	**Gene Littler** Doug Sanders/Bob Goalby	281 282	**Oakland Hills C.C.,** (South Course) Birmingham, Mich.	2,4

Date	Winner, Runner-Up	Score	Site	Entry
1962 (June)	**Jack Nicklaus** Arnold Palmer	283-71 283-74	**Oakmont C.C.,** Oakmont, Pa.	2,475
1963 (June)	**Julius Boros** Jacky Cupit Arnold Palmer	293-70 293-73 293-76	**The Country Club,** Brookline, Mass.	2,392
1964 (June)	**Ken Venturi** Tommy Jacobs	278 282	**Congressional C.C.,** Washington, D.C.	2,341
1965 (June)	**Gary Player** Kel Nagel	282-71 282-74	**Bellerive C.C.,** St. Louis, Mo.	2,271
1966 (June)	**Bill Casper, Jr.** Arnold Palmer	278-69 278-73	**Olympic Club,** (Lake Course) San Francisco, Calif.	2,475
1967 (June)	**Jack Nicklaus** Arnold Palmer	275 279	**Baltusrol G.C.,** (Lower Course) Springfield, N.J.	2,651
1968 (June)	**Lee Trevino** Jack Nicklaus	275 279	**Oak Hill C.C.,** (East Course) Rochester, N.Y.	3,007
1969 (June)	**Orville Moody** Deane Beman/Al Geiberger/Bob Rosburg	281 282	**Champions G.C.,** (Cypress Creek Course) Houston, Tex.	3,397
1970 (June)	**Tony Jacklin** Dave Hill	281 288	**Hazeltine National G.C.,** Chaska, Minn.	3,605
1971 (June)	**Lee Trevino** Jack Nicklaus	280-68 280-71	**Merion G.C.,** (East Course) Ardmore, Pa.	4,279
1972 (June)	**Jack Nicklaus** Bruce Crampton	290 293	**Pebble Beach G.L.,** Pebble Beach, Calif.	4,196
1973 (June)	**John Miller** John Schlee	279 280	**Oakmont C.C.,** Oakmont, Pa.	3,580
1974 (June)	**Hale Irwin** Forrest Fezler	287 289	**Winged Foot G.C.,** (West Course) Mamaroneck, N.Y.	3,914
1975 (June)	**Lou Graham** John Mahaffey	287-71 287-73	**Medinah C.C.,** (No. 3 Course) Medinah, Ill.	4,214
1976 (June)	**Jerry Pate** Tom Weiskopf/Al Geiberger	277 279	**Atlanta Athletic C.,** Duluth, Ga.	4,436
1977 (June)	**Hubert Green** Lou Graham	278 279	**Southern Hills C.C.,** Tulsa, Okla.	4,608
1978 (June)	**Andy North** J.C. Snead/Dave Stockton	285 286	**Cherry Hills C.C.,** Englewood, Colo.	4,897
1979 (June)	**Hale Irwin** Gary Player/Jerry Pate	284 286	**Inverness Club,** Toledo, Ohio	4,853
1980 (June)	**Jack Nicklaus** Isao Aoki	†272 274	**Baltusrol G.C.,** (Lower Course) Springfield, N.J.	4,812
1981 (June)	**David Graham** Bill Rogers/George Burns	273 276	**Merion G.C.,** (East Course) Ardmore, Pa.	4,946
1982 (June)	**Tom Watson** Jack Nicklaus	282 284	**Pebble Beach G.L.,** Pebble Beach, Calif.	5,255
1983 (June)	**Larry Nelson** Tom Watson	280 281	**Oakmont C.C.,** Oakmont, Pa.	5,039
1984 (June)	**Fuzzy Zoeller** Greg Norman	276-67 276-75	**Winged Foot G.C.,** (West Course) Mamaroneck, N.Y.	5,195
1985 (June)	**Andy North** Chen Tze-Chung/Denis Watson/Dave Barr	279 280	**Oakland Hills C.C.,** (South Course) Birmingham, Mich.	5,274
1986 (June)	**Raymond Floyd** Lanny Wadkins/Chip Beck	279 281	**Shinnecock Hills G.C.,** Southampton, N.Y.	5,410
1987 (June)	**Scott Simpson** Tom Watson	277 278	**Olympic Club,** (Lake Course) San Francisco, Calif.	§5,696

† Record Score * Denotes Amateur § Record Entry

1917 — An Open Patriotic Tournament was conducted by the USGA for the benefit of the American Red Cross at the Whitemarsh Valley Country Club, Philadelphia, Pa., June 20-22. Winner: Jock Hutchison, 292; runner-up: Tom McNamara, 299.

1942 — A Hale America Tournament was conducted by the USGA in cooperation with the Chicago District Golf Association and the Professional Golfers' Association of America for the benefit of the Navy Relief Society and the United Service Organization at Ridgemoor Country Club, Chicago, Ill., June 18-21. Winner: Ben Hogan, 271; runners-up: Jimmy Demaret and Mike Turnesa, 274.

87th U. S. Open

Championship Records

Amateurs: Champions — Francis Ouimet (1913); Jerome D. Travers (1915); Charles Evans, Jr. (1916); Robert T. Jones, Jr. (1923-26-29-30); John Goodman (1933).

Amateurs: Lowest 18-Hole Score — 65 by James B. McHale in third round in 1947, and James Simons in third round in 1971.

Amateurs: Lowest 72-Hole Scores — 282 by Jack Nicklaus in 1960; 283, James Simons in 1971.

Best Comebacks — 18 Holes: Jack Fleck in 1955 was nine strokes off the pace and came back to win.

36 Holes — Lou Graham in 1975 was 11 strokes behind.

54 Holes — Arnold Palmer in 1960 was seven strokes behind. John Miller in 1973 was six strokes behind.

63 Holes — Billy Casper was seven strokes behind Arnold Palmer with nine holes to play in 1966. Casper shot 32 on the incoming nine, Palmer shot 39.

Best Start by Champion — 63 by Jack Nicklaus in 1980.

Best Finish by Champion — 63 by John Miller in 1973. Second low is 65 by Arnold Palmer in 1960, Jack Nicklaus in 1967 and Fuzzy Zoeller in a playoff in 1984.

Champions Who Led All the Way — Only four have led after every round — Walter Hagen in 1914, Jim Barnes in 1921, Ben Hogan in 1953 and Tony Jacklin in 1970. Seven other champions have led or were in a tie all the way — Willie Anderson in 1903, Alex Smith in 1906, Charles Evans, Jr., in 1916, Tommy Bolt in 1958, Jack Nicklaus in 1972 and 1980, and Hubert Green in 1977.

Clubs Most Often Host — Baltusrol Golf Club, Springfield, N.J., and Oakmont Country Club, Oakmont, Pa., six times. Opens were played at Baltusrol in 1903, 1915, 1936, 1954, 1967 and 1980, and at Oakmont in 1927, 1935, 1953, 1962, 1973 and 1983. Oakland Hills Country Club, Birmingham, Mich., has been host to the Open five times, in 1924, 1937, 1951, 1961 and 1985.

Consecutive Winners — Five players: Willie Anderson (1903-04-05); John J. McDermott (1911-12); Robert T. Jones, Jr. (1929-30); Ralph Guldahl (1937-38) and Ben Hogan (1950-51).

Entry Record — 5,696 in 1987.

Finishes in First Ten — 18 by Jack Nicklaus. Walter Hagen finished in the first ten 16 times; Ben Hogan 15 times.

First Score in 60s — David Hunter, of Essex Country Club, West Orange, N.J., returned a card of 68 in the first round of the 1909 Championship. He finished with 313 and in a tie for 30th.

Foreign Winners — David Graham, of Australia, became the 20th foreign-born winner in 1981. However, 16 of the 20 had already emigrated to the United States before they won. The four overseas champions were Harry Vardon of England in 1900, Ted Ray of England in 1920, Gary Player of South Africa in 1965, and Tony Jacklin of England in 1970.

Foreign Players' Best 72-Hole Scores — 273 — David Graham in 1981; 274 — Isao Aoki in 1980; 276 — Greg Norman in 1984; 280 — Chen Tze-Chung, Denis Watson and Dave Barr in 1985; 281 — Tony Jacklin in 1970; 282 — Gary Player and Kel Nagle in 1965, Bobby Locke in 1948, Seve Ballesteros in 1987.

Highest Scores to Lead Field, 18 Holes — All-time high is 89 by Willie Dunn, James Foulis, and Willie Campbell in 1895. Since World War II, high is 71 in 1951, 1958, 1970 and 1972.

Highest Scores to Lead Field, 36 Holes — All-time high is 173 by Horace Rawlins in 1895. (This was a 36-hole Open.) Since World War II, high is 144 in 1951, 1955 and 1972.

Highest Scores to Lead Field, 54 Holes — All-time high is 249 by Stewart Gardner in 1901. Since World War II, high is 218 in 1951 and 1963.

Highest Scores to Lead Field, 72 Holes — All-time high is 331 by Willie Anderson and Alex Smith in 1901; Anderson won the playoff. More recent high is 299 by Sam Parks, Jr., in 1935. The post-World War II high is 293 by Julius Boros, Jacky Cupit and Arnold Palmer in 1963; Boros won the playoff.

Highest 72-Hole Score — Professional John Harrison, 393, in 1900.

Highest 36-Hole Cut — 155 in 1955 (low 50 and ties).

Lowest 9-Hole Score — 30 by Danny Edwards on the second nine of the second round in 1986; by Lennie Clements on the first nine of the third round in 1986; by Chip Beck on the second nine of the fourth round in 1986; by George Burns on the first nine of the second round in 1982; by Raymond Floyd on the first nine of the first round in 1980; by Tom Shaw in the first round and Bob Charles in the last round in 1971, both on the first nine; by Steve Spray on the second nine of the fourth round in 1968; by Ken Venturi on the first nine of the third round in 1964; by Arnold Palmer on the first nine of the final round in 1960; and by amateur James B. McHale, Jr., on the first nine of the third round in 1947.

Lowest Round — 63 by Jack Nicklaus and Tom Weiskopf (first round) over the Lower Course of the Baltusrol Golf Club, Springfield, N.J., in 1980; by John Miller (final round) at Oakmont Country Club, Oakmont, Pa., in 1973.

Lowest First Round — 63 by Jack Nicklaus and Tom Weiskopf, at the Baltusrol Golf Club, Springfield, N.J., in 1980.

Lowest Second Round — 64 by Tommy Jacobs, Congressional Country Club, Bethesda, Md., in 1964; by Rives McBee, Olympic Club, San Francisco, in 1966.

Lowest Third Round — 64 by Ben Crenshaw, Merion Golf Club, Ardmore, Pa., in 1981; by Keith Clearwater, Olympic Club, San Francisco, in 1987.

Lowest Fourth Round — 63 by John Miller, Oakmont (Pa.) Country Club, in 1973.

Lowest First 36 Holes — 134 by Jack Nicklaus in 1980 and Chen Tze Chung in 1985.

Lowest Last 36 Holes — 132 by Larry Nelson in 1983.

Lowest First 54 Holes — 203 by George Burns in 1981 and Chen Tze Chung in 1985. 204 by Jack Nicklaus and Isao Aoki in 1980.

Lowest Last 54 Holes — 204 by Jack Nicklaus in 1967.

Lowest 36-Hole Cut — 146 in 1980 and 1985 (low 60 and ties); 147 in 1960 (low 50 and ties).

Lowest 72-Hole Scores — 272 - Jack Nicklaus (63-71-70-68) in 1980; 273 - David Graham (68-68-70-67) in 1981; 274 - Isao Aoki (68-68-68-70) in 1980; 275 - Jack Nicklaus (71-67-72-65) in 1967; and Lee Trevino (69-68-69-69) in 1968.

Most Consecutive Birdies — Six by George Burns, who birdied the second through the seventh holes in the second round at Pebble Beach (Calif.) Golf Links in 1982.

Most Consecutive Opens — Gene Sarazen teed off in 31 successive Opens from 1920 through 1954 (no Championship 1942-45 because of World War II). Arnold Palmer teed off in 31 consecutively from 1953 through 1983. Jack Nicklaus has played in 31 consecutive Opens (1957-1987).

Most Victories — Four men have won four times: Willie Anderson (1901-03-04-05), Robert T. Jones, Jr. (1923-26-29-30), Ben Hogan (1948-50-51-53), Jack Nicklaus (1962-67-72-80).

Most Times Runner-up — Sam Snead, Robert T. Jones, Jr., Arnold Palmer and Jack Nicklaus, four times each.

Most Decisive Victories — 11 strokes - Willie Smith in 1899. Nine strokes - Jim Barnes in 1921.

Most Sub-Par Rounds in Career — 30 by Jack Nicklaus; 18 by Ben Hogan; 17 by Sam Snead and Lee Trevino.

Most Rounds Under 70 in Career — 25 by Jack Nicklaus; 15 by Arnold Palmer; Ben Hogan had 14.

Most Strokes on One Hole — Ray Ainsley took 19 strokes on the par-four sixteenth in the second round at the Cherry Hills Club, Englewood, Colo., in 1938.

Oldest Champion — Raymond Floyd was 43 years, eight months and 11 days old, when he won in 1986; Ted Ray was 43 years, four months and 16 days old, when he won in 1920; Julius Boros, the third oldest, was 26 days younger than Ted Ray on the day he won the Championship in 1963.

Pace-Setters with Largest Leads, 18 Holes — Five strokes - Tommy Armour in 1933.

Pace-Setters with Largest Leads, 36 Holes — Five strokes - Willie Anderson in 1903.

Pace-Setters with Largest Leads, 54 Holes — Seven strokes - Jim Barnes in 1921.

Poorest Start for Champion — The all-time high is 91 by Horace Rawlins in 1895. The post-World War II high is 76 by Ben Hogan in 1951 and Jack Fleck in 1955.

Poorest Finish for Champion — All-time high is 84 by Fred Herd in 1898. the post-World War II high is 75 by Cary Middlecoff in 1949.

Youngest Champion — John J. McDermott was 19 years, 10 months and 14 days old when he won in 1911.